ACHIEVE WHAT YOU WANT

Srilekha Mundla

WOW Book Publishing™

Achieve what you want

First Edition Published by Srilekha Mundla

WOW Book Publishing™

The purpose of this book is to educate and entertain. The views and opinions expressed in this book are that of the author based on her personal experiences and education. The author does not guarantee that anyone following the techniques, suggestions, ideas or strategies will become successful.

The author shall neither be liable nor responsible for any loss or damage allegedly arising from any information or suggestion in this book.

DEDICATION

I wrote this book to discover my brain and my awareness. I would like to give my children some hope that they can achieve anything they want if they believe in themselves.

I dedicate this book to an individual, or rather a group of individuals, who I imagined in my brain were supporting me and cheering for me in my small wins. I owe them lifelong love and gratitude.

With love
Srilekha

Tablf of Contents

About the Author

The author is an educated middle-aged woman. An immigrant with brown skin who never believed in herself. Always complaining and adjusting with life. She never believed that she is talented and beautiful, inside and out. She was always looking for acceptance to prove her worth. She knew only to complain and cry. But when she believed in herself, her confidence rose, she looked more attractive, and people respected her more. Now, she doesn't care about what others think or what they are doing; she cares about what brings her joy and peace by being herself. She likes to be a role model to other beautiful, brown women that believe in themselves. She fits in this perfect world with love and joy in her heart. She wants **others who have low confidence** to believe the same.

Foreword

Why this book and what is the benefit to me and others? This is a story of my awareness of my world. Each of us sees things differently based on our experiences of life.

Believing and loving yourself are so important. Faith, God, kindness, and compassion all come only after you love yourself completely. You have to accept the fact that you are a masterpiece, no one was like you before and no one will ever be like you.

Everything is noise and others' opinions. What feels right to you? That is right.

You don't fight with anyone, you always fight with yourself, your beliefs are set up by society, culture, and family. Be strong, even if you are vulnerable, be authentic in that vulnerability. That gives you power. You radiate light and you feel that light and other people can see your light. You bring change in yourself, you become a role model to others. If you don't believe, say 1000 times every day to your brain that you believe in you. That can be soul, consciousness. You evolve to a higher consciousness and bring change.

Acknowledgements

I was looking for individuals to acknowledge or other areas of research who have helped me to write this book. This book is merely my own experience of life. My inner pain helped me to transform into the person I am today. I also acknowledge that this is my awareness. I don't know the other side of the stories. I am not curious to know now, like I used to be.

The Universe/God gives limited awareness for a reason. Awareness is such a vast thing; it is an ocean and ours is a drop in that ocean. That drop of awareness has to help another individual a little bit. We are connected to individual awareness and become conscious. Consciousness has to be pure, we always try to be conscious of the outside world and we forget our soul consciousness. When you are pure in consciousness, you speak the truth and you are the same person inside out.

We come to this earth with consciousness and we take with us some consciousness. The Universe/God does not discriminate between good and bad. His consciousness is unconditional love and he mixes all the consciousness which we take with us, splits it equally and sends it back again to earth. Some people have to clean their consciousness and work hard a lot more than others which is based on their karma. Be kind and gentle to each other. If you don't, you will have an unclean consciousness and that is hard work and painful to correct. If we are a good soul, we give back the learning and leave with peace. My acknowledgement is more acceptance.

Note to the Reader

The information the author has shared is based on the author's personal experiences and awareness. The author and the publisher make no warranties, either expressed or implied, concerning the accuracy, applicability, effectiveness, reliability, or suitability of the contents. If you wish to apply or follow the advice or recommendations mentioned herein, you take full responsibility for your actions. The author and publisher of this book shall in no event be held liable for any direct, indirect, incidental, or consequential damages arising directly or indirectly from the use of any of the information contained in this book.

All content is for information only and is not warranted for content accuracy or any other implied or explicit purpose.

CHAPTER 1

Believe in yourself, it is your responsibility

Believe in yourself. It's your responsibility. Yes, it is your responsibility to believe in yourself. I used to think, okay, someone will come and help me. I wanted to become a successful person. I wanted to earn more money. I wanted to be happy. I wanted to have an abundant life. So, I would look for people who would come to help me, but nobody will come to help you. It's your responsibility, it's you alone who can fix your life. If you know this truth, then you are far ahead of anybody else. If you're working on your business, if you're working on a new skill, if you're taking care of your body, your health, your mind, your soul it's your responsibility, don't blame your failings on others.

That fact took me years to realize, that it was my responsibility. I should not be blaming my failings on others. It's your responsibility to be confident. When people are putting, you down, it's your responsibility to stand up for yourself. If you have dreams and desires, it's your responsibility to stand up for them and achieve them. Maybe if you have a spouse who is taking advantage of you, and then he's putting his way of thinking and his limitations on you, don't think from his brain. It's your responsibility to take control of your life. So, if you realize this fact, that's where the change starts.

So, I will tell you a small story of my own life. So, I always think, okay, I have too much faith in God. I always think that, okay, God is going to send somebody who can help me, who can lift me up? Yes, he did send somebody, it was me and my strength. He didn't send anybody. I just pulled that from my soul, from my mind. And when I started doing that, I started believing in myself. That is nothing but confidence. So, when you are down and looking for help, it's just that you alone can save yourself. And it is your responsibility to save yourself. That's how you transform your life. Last year, when I started taking responsibility believing in myself and I was not looking forward to anyone to come into my life and save me, not even my husband, I started learning, I started transforming and I started taking action.

Anything can be changed with laser-focus.

Anything can be changed with laser-focus. Anyone can become good at what they're doing by persistent action. You might have heard this from spiritual leaders and self-development gurus. They say "Live in the present moment." To be in the present moment means to be focused, whatever you're doing.

If you're learning a new skill, be focused. If you are doing work, be focused.

If you are laser-focused, anything can be changed in your life and that is the power of concentration. We have more advantages with technology, information at our fingertips and equally also many distractions. But if you work on your focus, you can do wonders, you improve your listening skills, and your curiosity improves. When you have that passion to grow, these are all interconnected. Maybe in the English language, they use different words. But you know, when you look at it, everything is connected. The only point here is to be focused. So, whatever the work you're doing, if you're cooking food, taking care of children, learning a new skill, or brushing your teeth, be focused.

When I came to America in 2000 there were no smart phones, I printed directions on paper for maps and then drove all around. Now everything is in the palm of your hand, with iPhones and Androids and the internet. Today you can access information at the touch of a button, it takes seconds to find something out. So the problem is not a scarcity of knowledge, it's having the focus to know what to choose and having the discipline to follow your choice. This is the only thing between the person who is successful and who can make it happen.

The difference between a successful person and a person who is struggling is discipline to focus. And social media is one of the major culprits that forms a distraction to focus. How often have you found yourself consumed by these thoughts...What did my friend post? How many likes did I get? All these thoughts are distractions. I repeat again, if you are laser-focused if you are living in that present moment, then you can achieve anything and everything you want. You have to teach that to your children because the next coming generations have focus deficiencies. I have heard this recently; new generation solutions are going to be the problems for the next generations. That's so true right now, we have technology, we have, everything at our fingertips, and with that technology, the distractions have increased in You're not able to focus when there are so many distractions and you have less focus which means you can't achieve much. So, keep this in mind, it's your responsibility to have that laser-focus and believe in yourself.

We all are made the same. It took forty-five years to understand this. I don't count the first 10 years of my life because we don't remember much from the first 10 years.

There are some people born rich, I don't deny that. But that richness has come from someone's sacrifice or someone's effort or consciousness. Their ancestors might have lived their life with focus and the best planning for future generations; they might have achieved that success because they believed in themselves.

Whatever the wealth they had, they passed on to their generations. It has started somewhere.

I realize now, no one's opinion of beauty has a standard. Beauty always comes from inside. We are all beautiful and that is a reflection of how we behave with other people.

It is our eyes which see beauty in others. So, I always say that when people give compliments, "you are beautiful", it's not them who is beautiful, it's you who is looking for beauty in them.

So, what I'm going to say is that we all are made the same.

Same thing with effort and talent everybody has got 24 hours.

Everybody has got the same brains, organs and blood. The difference is the colour of the skin based on how close your ancestors lived, whether they lived close to, or father from, the equator. Every person, when they become old, they get wrinkles. Superiority is given by human consciousness and that is carried by human minds from generations.

We all are made the same.

The only difference is how focused you can be.

Focus is something we can work on, so other than that beauty, colour, these are all the things made by human brains like make-up stories. We made that story and we believe it for generations and keep on believing.

So, if the other person is speaking intelligently that means they worked on it. They read and studies and therefore gained more knowledge. It doesn't mean that they are born with that talent. Maybe the only difference would be that to achieve the same level you have to read and study multiple times to grasp the same knowledge because your attention is not as good as his attention, you're getting distracted and they are focused. So, they understand it the first time. But we all are made the same, if there is one thing you must teach your kids and the next generations that we all are made the same. You are same as any other human; you think they are better than you because of limitations created in your mind or by listening to others negative thoughts. We are all gifted in some way or another.

What are our gifts and what are we capable of? We need to work on them and say to ourselves we are all the same.

People pull you down is a wrong heading.

I started this chapter titled as 'people pull you down', I was so wrong. Others pull you down if you give them a chance. If you are in charge of your mind, no human can pull you down, at least mentally. We put those limitations, what do they think about me?

What about my family and friends? Does that matter to you, what others think of you? What do you think of yourself? Do you think that you are weak? Do you think you can't achieve what you want?

It is your thoughts that have maximum impact on you. When do you know how to control those and win them? Then you win the whole world. No one has time to think about others other than their family and their circle.

There are millions and billions of people in the world. If someone doesn't like you and you feel that impacting on you, then don't dwell on that one human.

There is a reason for everything in the Universe. If the person behaves badly with you, it has nothing to do with you. It's their bad karma making them act the way they are acting. Move on, God is showing and telling you "It's not worth your time my child." Imagine closing that thought.

Why are they like that? What did I do to them? Imagine after closing that room of thought you lock it and throw the key in the deep sea or forest. Don't ever look for that key!! Let the Universe handle your pain. There is law in the Universe. It looks from every angle. I used to wonder why one person was in so much pain? God has no mercy. I realized it's the law. You are you. What is your true nature? You never change that because someone did something bad to you. If you are a loving human being, don't make yourself cruel. Forgive and forget, including yourself and the people around you that did you harm, but never forget the lessons you learned in that experience.

It's a boomerang. Our consciousness travels in the Universe. It affects you and your actions affect others. No evil, no good. It is just consciousness. Your feelings may be nothing to others.

Pain is real, if someone is screaming with pain you try to help, not hurt more. That is the sign of a good person. The pain is inevitable in human life, but suffering is optional.

Desires

Desires are nothing but purpose in life. I live a successful life. What success means for some people may be different for others; to some success is money, for others success is family, happiness, love or fame In my point of view, success is fulfilling your desire.

We all come to this earth and then we have a desire which we feel we have to achieve. That desire, if you fulfil it, that is a success.

So,when I say desire, that desire to me means many things.I want to buy things and go to different countries. That's a desire, but not the type of desire I am meaning. I am talking about the desire that pushes you. For example, you can say I get up and go to work and make a paycheck, is that my desire? Yes, that is your desire to live a comfortable life and support your family.

Why am I doing this? Your children/family is your purpose.

Some people who have changed the lives of other people and their desires, did not speak of their own desires.

Instead they showed it in their actions, like Martin Luther King, Mahatma Gandhi, and Mother Teresa.

These people desired to see that others get the freedom they deserve. That was their desire.

Not everyone becomes a Martin Luther King or a Mother Teresa or a Mahatma Gandhi, but we have our desires, the small desires where we like to take care of our family. People like to build wealth so that their children are happy. That is their desire. That is their purpose. Some people love is their desire to others always be loved by others.

It's their desire. Desires are your purpose. So, work on those desires, the long-term desires, not the short-term ones, the long-term desires where you feel again and again, and feel that is intuition or your call. What is intuition? The sudden bulb, which glows in your brain and your heart, no, that is not intuition. Your heart will tell you, and you are drawn naturally towards that go and take that action, go and do step out of your fears... that will be told by your intuition. And that intuition is strong when you are connected and aligned with the Universe or God because you live in harmony with the Universe and God, you speak the truth and you live with love. So that takes you to the right path. You don't have to look for your purpose,you are already fulfilling it.

With your long-term desire there is nothing wrong or right. Some people are working hard for their families and they want to leave that legacy. That is their desire/ purpose.

Kindness is not weakness

Kindness is a behavior; it is the act of life and quality of good human nature. This quality, if it is applied to others, is appreciated in society but we forget that we come first. We forget to apply kindness to us but we do it to everyone.

When we think that we have to apply this quality to ourselves, we are judged as selfish. We are run over by every human being you encounter in life. We act as loving humans and the others take advantage of that quality to their advantage.

Some people feel that they are not able to express feelings and lead a depressed life and suffer from anxiety. What do others think? Should you even give a damn what others think? How are you feeling inside? Do you feel that you are heard? Do you feel that you are respected? Are you able to make decisions with your brain? I was talking to someone today; we Indians live like that. Really!! This is a story I read in a book, about a nurse who was treating patients who were terminally ill and were close to death and were on death bed. The nurse asked the what the one thing was that they would change in their life if they could go back in time. Each of the patients surprisingly gave the same answer; lived my life with courage.

Life is a gift and humans have wisdom. Culture, society, and Family only come after your soul. Take care of that beautiful soul. Each soul has different energies and all of them radiate their own beauty. Be conscious every second of your life. Once the body leaves consciousness travels in the Universe and merges with higher consciousness. Each of us came with a purpose. That purpose need not be great but is important.

The purpose could be taking care of your body, your family, or your contribution to society. You could be like a drop of water in the ocean but that drop is needed. Don't leave your core qualities to fit in somewhere. You will lose your identity.

If something is telling you it's not right, and you are fighting against it, that is your intuition telling you that the soul is not happy. You don't need to express and share with hundreds of people and get hundreds of opinions. Just feel how you are feeling.

Don't get manipulated and confused. There are possibilities of others manipulating you due to the media.

Sit down and meditate, you find answers slowly. Don't run from situations, be alert, have control of your mind and with that strength raise your consciousness. That is the only end goal for any person.

CHAPTER 2

Exercise and healthy food (the body is the only vehicle and it has to become strong).

Exercise and eat healthy food. Yes. This is a very small subject and we all know this. Some people ignore this saying that life is short, others make resolutions every day and feel guilty when they check their weight, see health reports, or do not look good on social media.

We all know that we have to exercise and eat healthy food. Even my 15-year-old son knows that he needs to exercise and go to the gym.

.So, this knowledge is not something new, but I will tell you how it helped me. The past 2 years, before this book, I transformed my life,every phase of it. Spiritually, physically, mentally, financially. It just happened with daily exercise. By doing exercise, I built my endurance and my capacity to do more work without being tired.

Food is the fuel that gives energy, don't eat just for the sake of taste. Be extremely conscious and mindful of what you are putting in your mouth. Humans are evolved animals only because of our consciousness. Take responsibility for your health. Did you know the gut is the second nervous system. Your thoughts, your anger, your desires, and your energy are based on the food you eat.

Imagine your body as a car and suppose you want to go to a certain destination, your car has to be running, right? Destinations are our goals.

I lost 35 pounds by doing yoga and walking. I felt my body become light. If you exercise and eat right you look younger and healthy, all those things that are an additional benefit. But for me this is the real strength exercise gave me:

I am an introvert, a person who has fear for everything, who is always dependent on a parent or a spouse, and who always listens to other people. From that person I became a confident person through excersise. The mind and body are connected,physical strength is necessary to get mental strength, and that physical strength comes from exercise.

There are no excuses for not doing exercise. I make sure I exercise my body and I see that strength in me with that exercise.

Rituals

Rituals changed my life. Doing the same thing at the same time helps. So, if you create those rituals as early as possible in your life, such as a morning ritual and/or evening ritual every day at the same time, such as, waking up, working out, and doing meditation at the same time then you don't get that secondary thought of, okay, what do I do next? You know subconsciously this is the timing you've been doing this activity. So let me finish this first. Once you create that habit, you can't stop it. If you wont even do a single day; you feel something is missing. I've been doing it for the past two years. I transformed. I never feel bored and I enjoy doing it and it's become a part of my life. It's my ritual, no matter what, I just do that.

Preparing for the day the day before, breathing exercises, making the bed…these are all the rituals that you can introduce in your life. Kids love to do things like their parents so make some time to create family rituals. Having rituals in my life has helped me to transform my life and will help you too.

Our whole life is based on habits. You can build a life based on habits. Your life is systemized. You don't have to think much to make choices. If you use less energy on day-to-day work, the rest you can use to be more creative and help others. So simple, but very profound. You can build your life on either the good side or the bad side. With the same habits, you can be a drug addict, or social media addict, with the same habits you can exercise and eat healthily. This looks very small but a person's whole life depends on habits.

Rituals are carried on for generations, family rituals, country rituals, religious rituals etc. Interesting, isn't it? My mom said something which resonated with me, she said "even thoughts are like habits," if you think negatively if you think about the past. The same thoughts you create again. If you consciously stop the thought, you can let it go. I exercise in my rituals because the body is the only vehicle for life. We focus on eating tasty food, the same way we have to build that happiness in exercising. Run, walk, do yoga and make it a habit. Not to impress others but to be a role model to your family and your soul.

I have seen most military people succeed in life. This happens because they learn habits in the military and they continue doing them afterwards. One ritual is very hard for me, that is taking a cold shower in winter, everyday my brain fights and says no, take a warm bath, it is very cold outside. I tell my brain, shut up, I am in charge and I am in the cold-water shower.

My whole family loves chicken and meat, while I am a vegetarian, however I cook the meat to sustain my family but I don't eat it . It's a choice I made two years ago and I stick to it. When people said they are vegetarian, I used to ask them, how do you live without eating meat? I can leave anything in food but not meat. I created the habit of eating vegetarian food and I am loving it. It's all habits and how bad you want that in your life.

If I can do it, anyone can do it. You don't need will-power once the habit is activated. You do it without your knowledge and conscious effort.

Exercise builds inner strength

When I started exercising, I started seeing change. Exercise makes your body and mind more conscious and alert.

As soon as I get up, I do yoga and then in the evening I walk for an hour. The exercise is a must for anyone who likes to achieve something in their life. Exercise builds inner strength.

Our body is the only vehicle we have. After 40 yrs. exercise is more for mental strength.

It's all about mental and physical strength. We all know that we have to exercise every day but we don't do it because we are lazy or don't feel like doing it. All internal hormones and amino acids are elevated only with exercise which helps us to think better and work better without becoming tired.

There are days in my life, on social media, people unnecessarily hated me and started mocking me every day with memes, like saying I am a baby Elephant,

I didn't know whom to ask for help. They were helping and hurting me badly with memes.

I used to feel, I am an introvert and shy person. I talk less to people and on top of it, I have my limitations.

I have an accent and I am not as equal as the person who was born and brought up in the USA.

I was taking all that humiliation and being nice even though they were hurting me. It took almost 2 years. I played their game and one day I decided enough is enough.

You get strength in two ways; one is an exercise with body and mental strength, and other one is financial, when you are capable of earning money.

We all have only a certain amount of focused time. The difference between a successful and unsuccessful person is that focused energy. That energy is gained with exercise. Lethargy and fatigue are common. You reduce fatigue with continuous routine workouts.

Beauty boosts confidence

Beauty always boosts confidence. Don't work only on beauty. Skin gets wrinkly with age and you lose muscle as you grow old. It is the confidence you get when you have strength. Think like an extra boost of confidence. The real beauty in any human comes with wisdom and how you treat the other person. That is the real beauty. Kindness and wisdom always win compared to a pretty face, great body with wicked nature and no focus.

When we talk about kindness or focus, the only senses that have to be alert are the ears and be present in that moment. Being present in the moment is such a small thing but it makes a world of difference in human life. Just don't be eager to spit out the knowledge and wisdom you have got to show your intelligence. Just listen and try to understand their point of view and then talk. True beauty comes with listening ears. The beauty of the body is important only to keep the body healthy and give the energy to focus. Other People's standards of beauty have no value, if you feel that you need to change the way you look then work on it. if you feel that way then change, if you don't, enjoy and love the way you are. It was a long process and I did not put on weight not because I had to look like a model or something else. I like to be thin and eat light food because I eat heavy. My focus levels are low and I am not that alert. The gut is the second brain, when you are consuming food that needs lots of energy to digest, the energy to the brain is not sufficient.

The nerve which has direct contact with the gut and brain is the vagus nerve.

Monks who fast for many days the only reason they do is to focus. If you like to test yourself, eat food which is very easily digestible and eat a heavy meal. Try to focus one hr after your meal. You will see a bigger difference. Life is small, we have to make most of it when we are alive.

Our food and eating habits play a major role in day-to-day life. Those smaller details give a bigger impact on your life and your success. The additional benefits are you look young and fewer health issues. Time and energy are the only things we have. Time is not controlled by us. The other thing which we can control is our energy. When we know how to control it, why not give it a try?

CHAPTER 3

The four most important virtues

Integrity

What is Integrity? Integrity doesn't mean society standards Integrity means more than that. Integrity means you say and act what you preach. Integrity means directly or indirectly you don't hurt others. Integrity means always speak the truth even though it hurts. You are the same public and private, that is integrity. Love is a form of integrity.

There is no judgement in love. I act for my benefit and my fun. If it helps the other person that is positive, if it doesn't, I shouldn't show myself as a bad human in front of society. That is not integrity.

The other person is sharing everything. Let me have fun with their personal information. That is not integrity.

A Person with integrity mostly shows his integrity with his actions. Public figures, Spiritual leaders who give great speeches on the stages and talk about the people lack integrity. Their private lives have no integrity. They don't look into their life but they like to build that public persona. This was life only to some public figures a few decades back but now anyone can do this using social media. Introspections are very important. The Younger generation has one more perspective, my body is young and I can do whatever I want and check to become noble and good when I get old. It never happens, you have to build these habits from a young age. People are so used to the fake, if you post a negative post no one likes that. Humans have both aspects in their lives. Be true to yourself. Be true to your family and society. Be real, be authentic, Be you. You live with integrity if you have basic standards. One basic standard is to treat the other person the same way you like to be treated. This one standard is enough to live a life with integrity. Everything will follow with one basic standard.

If you don't have integrity, your children who are watching you learn this by watching their parents. It's ok to live in the house someway and we have to act differently when we are in public. No standards and ultimately it is going to hurt society. They learn Hypocrisy. The last thing you learn about integrity is respect. When you respect others there is no need to put extra effort to learn integrity.

Integrity and respect go hand and hand.

Harmony

Harmony is so important in life partnerships, if no harmony leads to unhappiness and depression.

Harmony is not only about doing things together; Harmony means what are my partner's goals and how can we improve to have a better life? Cooking and watching movies and taking care of kids are not only examples of harmony. Listening to your partner is the first step toward a harmonious life. Your goals are my goals, it's our goals, it's our family goals, just not financially, Spiritually and physically.

Most People are living together for society, for families and children. If they like to come out of that worst life, the cultural conditioning pushes them into it. Animals are living with more freedom than humans.

You don't expect 100% harmony at least if you are harmonious 80%, you can live a happy life. If that is not there that family turned out very unorganized with children with no respect and no proper guidance. In India, arranged marriages are mostly for generations. How did their parents, grandparents and great-grandparents live? It is important to see that. Kids inherit the behavior. People are blessed with this type of harmony. Sometimes, harmony can be built if there is mutual respect and they grow together. Growth is so important because it helps to look forward to tomorrow. A person who feels authoritative in the relationship will sit down and talk to his or her partner and try to change their habits. If you eat super healthy, exercise and are positive in your behavior, still you can be sick mentally if you don't live a harmonious life. If you don't find that partnership at home you look outside.

Most of the unfaithfulness happening in this world is happening because families are disconnected mentally. 99% of the time men or women are attached to their parents, friends, and siblings in their middle age. That midlife crisis is due to a lack of harmony in their partnerships.

Communicating, understanding and thinking at deeper levels help to solve these problems.

Couple power

The understanding between two humans is very important in any growth. In any relationship, it starts with love and keeps growing that relationship with respect. The human soul can feel that more than love.

In cultures, where women are seen just as a person to feed the family, sleep next to a husband and show the love how the spouse wanted them to show. Those families will go into severe distress.

Kids learn by watching their parents. The couples have to be equal partners and sit down and discuss their family, social life, financial life, and spirituality. It cannot be 100% ideal but few of them have to match.

I have seen in my culture they teach to adjust with life. How long one can do that? One day, people get tired and sick of the adjustments they make in life. Some things we cannot be masters but we can learn everything online.

Blessed this time to be born with knowledge if the humans are still unhappy and not learning they are the cursed ones.

God doesn't come down and say live your life like this. No human life is perfect. Each of them had their level of problems or sorrows. Where is unhappiness and how do we fix this? Instead of running away from a problem facing it, communicate to solve those problems. There are so many divorces, and cheatings happening in this world because you don't care about other people. What can I get from him /her? If that is not working, let's keep our mouths shut and lead our lives for children, society, and families.

One friend said last week that after complaining about her spouse 'She is divorced and she is still unhappy" Really!! I asked her "Are you completely happy in your marriage at least she is figuring it out and dares to be truthful to herself"? Appreciate that quality.

Teach children to not run away from the problem, stand there, listen to other humans and feel how the other person is treating them, express, and communicate.

If you learn this at home, I feel that you do well in the world, work or business.

Listening is love, Listening is respect. Few people follow this. You can change your entire life when you start with this one skill. You connect to them forever.

Self-discipline

I struggle with self-discipline, it has to do with the internal fight, nothing externally. We try to fix it with motivational videos, inspiration and affirmation. That helps a little bit but does not last long. Internally you solve one problem or the environment is changed then self-discipline is easy. There is no strong barrier.

We work on habits and change our routines and work on the subconscious mind. We can change a little bit. Self-discipline is going to be an uphill battle.

The easy way is to change the environment and be at the moment. Self-discipline is always momentary. That moment and the next moment and the next. It has become a habit. Once it becomes a habit, it is hard to work and change that habit. Be careful of the choices you make at that moment.

Even though we build routines we make decisions based on that moment. Always be present at the moment which helps a lot in self-discipline. The self-discipline, good habits, routines to make our surroundings a clean and happy place. Human life is a journey to hold each other's hands without hurting other souls, honest communication, speaking the truth all are pure energies. We clean each other's paths and carry good or bad with our souls.

That good and bad travels with our consciousness and energy merge into higher energy. It is like a goal. We focus on the goal, take action and measure. One day we will reach our goal. Life is also the same way measured with energy, being present and looking at the future, in the future if you only consider the body then you are not looking at the bigger picture there is something bigger than that that is soul.

The human goal has to take care of soul energy.

Self-discipline is being present at the moment and looking at the bigger picture the goal is to take care of souls' energy and that is the true wealth that passes with life after life after and gives moksha.

Kindness matters

Kindness matters. People think kindness is a weakness. It is strength.

You are showing with your actions of kindness to others that you need to change.

I am kind, People take advantage of me, I request and beg and be mocked and bullied by others.

I stand still like a rock. Let them do what they like to do. I was in a situation where people had power and I became vulnerable at certain times.

They took advantage of my vulnerability. They helped me a little bit by showing me the path and motivating me. They were treating me very badly. I could feel that from time to time. I shut my mouth because someone was listening and supporting me to become financially stable. It was also hurting my self-esteem. If I open my mouth, they would say be grateful. Being grateful has to start with your soul and body. You have to be grateful to your soul, Atma before you are to other humans.

Kindness and gratefulness to others come only after you respect your space.

I tell you a story, Gandhi didn't have a great physique, He never wore fancy clothes, He always talked about Ahimsa and kindness. When Gandhi entered the court, the British judge stood up and respected him.

Gandhi showed respect for himself and he respects people with love and kindness. The whole world respected him. He was strong mentally. He became a symbol.

Kindness doesn't mean that someone runs over you, you let go.

You stand up for yourself and say stop. Kindness also means if weak ones are humiliated and bullied by others, you stand up for them.

As humans are progressing with new inventions and discoveries.

The basic human character is lacking. Don't confuse kindness and gratefulness with humility and let go. You stand up for yourself and the weaker ones surrounding you. That is real kindness.

CHAPTER 4

The root cause of suffering

Ignorance

Humans are social creatures, we always try to fit in. We are happy if we can make decisions without caring about others. We say that but we don't live.

Always live to fit in. Some people who are strong and kind and stand up for themselves become true leaders.

For others who are interested in teaching a lesson to others, let's look into our own life. We have so much baggage, open our mouths, lie, never speak the truth and are ready to advise others.

We have standards and these standards and rules are the number one reason for depression and anxiety. Governments impose rules, society imposes rules, and families impose rules on top of all our minds impose rules on our life. What happens to the soul? It dies inside without expressing itself. All the time we fear. Most of the stuff happens due to ignorance and lack of knowledge and it runs in generations and families suffer big time. Become a warrior, do that, do this. For what? Are you happy? If it brings you true joy, do it. Don't do that due to external pressures. Don't allow your mind to be a government to your body to impress others.

Look at the animals, they don't know the language and they know only hunger and love and they live happily.

Humans feel jealous, hatreds. Animals are blessed.

In this covid time you ever heard animals given any covid protection, no masks, they are not given any covid vaccines, even though every person in a household is affected?

No animals are wearing masks. Humans are affected by pandemics. Nature can see happiness, love and respond to it. Animals have love and happiness, not humans. It is so sad but that is the truth.

When we are depressed, we get a dog or cat because they show pure love without expectations.

Can you believe we are reaching to other planets with our knowledge and wisdom and we show prejudice and bigotry toward each other based on color, accent, and race because we have to fit into the standards of society?

People who talk about love and compassion to millions and millions of people are killed by their own families.

On top of all these, movies and media always give ideas to the human brain and extra dose of negative injection.

These incidents happened here. What does the ignorant Human brain get out of it? You can do crime this way.

They repeat the same negative news on 10 other channels. There are so many positive happening shows that people get motivated and inspired by watching them. No one cares. When some crime happens, People are so busy recording and posting on social media instead of stepping forward to help.

Ask them to write positive quotes, ever ready to do that. Our ancestors planted trees looking forward to our children and their children's lives.

We don't have to go out and plant trees, just respect other humans.

Put yourself in their shoes and give one thought. What might they have undergone to behave the way they are doing? One compassionate thought changes the world, you don't need to work for charity, give money to others.

Be less judgmental and one thought of compassion before judging others. Be the change you want to see the world.

Limitations

To all the women with color or without color, don't look for support or help from people whom you don't know. Don't think the people are pure at heart and help you. If they help you, they look for their advantage first before they even think of helping you.

This has nothing to do with a negative or positive mindset. This is the world right now. Believe in yourself. That is only a mantra.

Failure after failure and my mind does not agree that I am incompetent but my failures show that I am fit for nothing. I asked for help on the internet. I didn't know them and I felt that if someone gives me some support, maybe I can become financially strong. They listened to me.

They started playing with my mind. I became a toy to them. They started controlling my mind. Two different types of mindsets, one was to be obedient and you are a bad woman and another message support and encourage me. They trained me through memes.

It went to a different level when a woman was vulnerable and shared her story and looked for help. Men don't care, they enjoy it. I was beaten down by my family.

My family was saying that I am not even worth the wages of a person who is working in Mcdonald's. Went to Dental School in India. I became a dentist and my life is worth nothing. I Cried, wiped my tears, took the motivation which was in social media and loved the person who supported me and hated the play they were playing with me but continued working day and night.

My belief was so low that I do all the work and I give the credit to the person whom I have never seen and talked to once.

His silence made me understand that he is there for me and that I should keep moving. This was not necessary, the only thing I needed was that I believe in myself or some support from my family.

I am wounded in this three-year play very badly. They wounded me internally.

I forgive everyone and I forgive myself. I promise that I will never be in that situation again. We have to be kind and respectful to ourselves first.

If You are not kind to yourself and love every human being, you deplete your energy.

Sometimes, I laugh because those who made fun of me and played did not play, they shared my karma and took some with them.

It's their ignorance. We learn lessons, get wounded and give karma to others and move on. That is life. I believe in oneness; this is a lesson. People don't have to do good all the time they do bad to you, it's a lesson to them to clear your path. Good and bad contribute to oneness.

CHAPTER 5

Increase productivity

Leverage

I am still working on this. I was born and brought up in India in a middle-class family. People who are born in developing countries value money a lot more than time. Money can be earned but once lost time cannot be gained back.

Entrepreneurship has to run in the family to get the knowledge or maintaining the knowledge through books.

People read books and finding out what is important in that book is very crucial. Few people have the art of catching the important thing and working on it. After the invention of the digital world, everything is at our fingertips.

When you open the internet, you can watch and listen at the same time without even reading it. In this knowledge pouring era, time is the biggest commodity.

Immigrants who come to this country live the American dream by converting rupees into dollars and are happy with the luxuries already there like big roads, a clean atmosphere and become content with life. When we leave our country and come to another country to live, we have to make a fortune. Not to live an ordinary life. A life where your generations cherish the sacrifice we did.

It's nothing wrong to dream big and showing jobs or inspiring people. I always tell my boys to be leaders who lead and help others. I always felt a secondary citizen because I have an accent and I had limiting beliefs; no other community will work with me. It is not true, it's all in my brain. Once I am out of that belief things started changing for me.

My mind imagined a character and I held on to him so tight and gave him so much power thinking that he was there walking behind me. That strength was mine but I was beaten down by society and family.

People get so annoyed if we talk to them but this person was there in silence listening to me for many years until I pulled strength out. For me, I imagined him as God.

Our brains are so conditioned by society and people around us who are willing to pull us down. We have to find courage and trust in external support. It has its repercussions but if I look at the good side his silence made me understand to move forward. He was tired because he was equally fighting. That imagination was in my mind. Once you know your strength, to be successful you need the right team willing to put the same effort and you need to learn how to delegate the stuff and some things are also done through technology. Be ready to spend time and learn the technology. Life is not that hard until we make it hard.

Coming out of our limitations, finding good people, and keeping good people by your side are challenging.

If you let go of things you can't control, be present, control emotions, think positive and be happy.

Leverage everything which you don't like to do and which saves you time to focus on a high dollar job.

It is a learned skill, it's not necessary to be in our DNA. I will tell you a little bit about India. In India, everyone who is living a middle-class life can afford servants in their house. They don't look at it as an extra expense. We lived a middle-class life and had three servants who were of our age but they were poor.

If my mom didn't have these kids as servants they would have been on the roads without food and no discipline. We used to play with those kids and they had jobs as servants and we enjoyed our childhood. Those kids turned out to be contractors and good citizens and well settled and grateful to my mom.

My mom spent her time enjoying it with us and her friends. She is smart. I realized that fact in my mid-forties. It is never too late; some lessons are hard but worth learning.

Time

Time is so important, Time is king. No one will ever defeat time.

Good or bad. It passes. If you want to make decisions, make them quick.

Once you pass the time. You don't get that people and time back. People think there is plenty of time in their life. Time is the only expensive commodity. Spend your time wisely. Be grateful to people who spend their time with you. Be strong, don't be a victim, take control, never beg, you don't even imagine your worth because we live in a small cocoon. If people put you down and you add more to it and start seeing you as less than you are worth.

Love everyone when you say love you genuinely love without judging and that love comes only after you. That is not selfish, it is selfless. It is protecting us. Our souls are so delicate we ignore them a lot to make others happy. You will be lost looking back. How you take care of your body, you get massages, do your nails, eat healthily, do exercise, the same way you take care of your precious soul/spirit.

If you are weak and tired of the environment, you become vulnerable at that time. You have to be extremely careful who you are vulnerable with. People say it's a strength to speak out. It is strength only if people love you. If they don't care and put you in situations where you are confused and create other vulnerable situations.

These preaching's are coming from my life experiences.

The core of any person won't change if you are a kind and loving person at your core, during that period of time you may hate them if people did wrong to you. When you become calm you understand their situation and let go.

Every human is different but kindness goes a long way. If anyone trusts you, speak the truth to them even though it hurts at that moment. In the long run, it gives peace to all.

Time is a very important thing and there is so much knowledge out there, what you like to take in and what you like to leave out is important. Not everyone makes wise decisions on this. It is very essential whom you are interacting with. It doesn't mean as a person but also in digital media.

What matters most is to cut the cords before you create that as a habit. That is emotional intelligence. I take everything in and ask my brain to process it. It does the process and also takes lots of energy to do that. It drains you.

Do you need that in life? That is the question to ask ourselves because time is limited.

Organization

Organizing gives clarity, it is a skill. Not everyone has it. It can be developed. It starts with breathing, thoughts, eating, lifestyle, parenting, house cleaning and financial planning.

Let's start with breathing. We think that breathing is such an involuntary act.

Life starts with breathing and ends when you stop breathing. It is important to check your breathing consciously. You will know whether you are shallow breathing or deep breathing. By conscious awareness of one of these involuntary acts, you can watch your focus. The one which we never even care much about has a huge impact on focus, living in the present moment and being conscious.

Try focusing on your breathing and start working on the task, you see your focus levels are high when you are doing that.

Let's talk about thoughts. Humans who have skills, knowledge and focus are still not able to succeed. The only reason is thought. They are stuck in past thoughts or future thoughts or getting unnecessary thoughts by watching useless media. That is the reason most people don't watch the news. There are so many positive things happening in life. We all continue with our lives because of that positivity, when we open the news channel, people talk about negativity and something bad has happened somewhere or bad is going to happen or it is happening right now.

It shows that our brains go into fear which drags the energy. Think with all that negative energy we were able to flourish so much. What if there was nothing negative that humans could achieve? Definitely more than what we have done.

Eating Habits, with little organizing we can cook homemade meals and eat healthy at home. Western civilization is so used to watching TV and Netflix and opening those cans and microwaving the food and finishing their meals. When the cancers hit their body then realization starts with holistic medicine. It is not required to make restaurant-style meals but we all have a choice with little planning. We can eat healthy home-cooked meals at home with organic foods and olive oil or any other high-quality oils.

With little planning, we can have a luxurious lifestyle with travel and spiritual education and learning instead of browsing unnecessary stuff and watching Netflix.

Parenting, Kids watch every aspect of our life consciously and subconsciously. It has a big impact on their life and their children's life and impacts the generations. This has to be done by both partners. It is better to be single and raise kids than with the wrong partners. It is also luck.

House cleaning and organizing, comes with passion with money you can leverage this nowadays. The last thing is financial planning. I was always thinking men have to do this. I was wrong because with good education women can do better than men. Again, it can be learned. I am still in the process.

CHAPTER 6

Confidence is the key and Rephrasing

Confidence is the key

I mentioned many times about confidence, and believing in yourself. When someone says, build your confidence. What exactly is confidence? When you are confident, what if others think you are proud, or you have an ego? First of all, being confident means others never come into the picture. Others have to be out of your mind. No need to impress others and no need to live for others. What feels right to your inner soul? Awareness of surroundings and making decisions.

In India people believe only fair skin is beautiful, Mom was so worried about my dark skin , i had to deal with mental trauma as a child.

I realized I am beautiful; I went to professional school and became a Dentist in India. I came to America with so many dreams. I was trying and failing and the teacher said I am incompetent to be a Dental hygienist.

Immigrants who are educated come to America and live looking for every dollar after twenty years is not acceptable.

Why did this happen? I didn't have enough confidence in myself? I believed in others instead of believing in myself. I went and asked a stranger for help. He listened to me and he tried his best to help me out with all his resources without talking to me. I am grateful for that. I fell in love with my growth and the support I was getting.

I showed my vulnerability and weakness. They started playing with me. It was a toll on my mental health.

Why did this happen? Again, lack of confidence. The whole pain revolves around me and my lack of confidence. I learned a blaming game. My mom did this to me, my husband did this to me, the teacher did this to me, a stranger did this to me. They didn't do anything; I was putting myself as a weak human and always afraid of others.

Today, I am at that point in my life. No more suffering, I take control. Things are not different, it takes time. I take abuse from others for a long time when I don't give myself a chance, people get upset. They think who is she? She is a confident woman who can handle anything life throws at her.

Rephrasing

There are millions of self-help books, Mine is going to be one more, why do you have to read this book?

I am going to tell you why. I came from India and I had so many limitations in my brain, limitations put on by others, limitations put on by myself and I had an unsuccessful life, all those things I could still achieve what I want.

When I told myself that's it. I am not believing any of the crap.

What I'm telling you is, it is not about who you are?

Maybe you have an accent and your English is bad. You are being played by people.

Someone is bullying you and then someone you are expecting never supports you nor is willing to listen to you. Your parents with their ignorance abused you. You're not loved, you're not respected, you're not appreciated.

And people who are in your life just take everything from you. With all these drawbacks, you still can make your dreams come true.

I am a successful investor and achieved more than I ever expected. To make this happen, I have to go through illusions, imagine a person and talk to him and gain strength thinking that he is there for me.

I imagined him as God and loved him to death.

From that I created my strength and started working.

The only thing you need to have been to believe in yourself and how you get it when you are in a cocoon. It starts with taking action.

I never cared about money. Money gives you strength.

If you are in your forties, fifties, sixties or seventies. I see some people in their nineties and they say we are ninety years young.

Age is just a number. The body is the vehicle, time is your buddy, you only need energy and focus to make anything happen in your favour. For all this to run in your favour, always love in your heart and smile on your face then rest leave that to the universe. I speak to trees; it is so funny. I do that. I will write one more book on that.

Take responsibility for anything in your life, completely responsible. We don't have to be submissive. Be you. Kindness and gratefulness to your soul. We don't take any wealth with us when we leave this body but you take one thing.

If you ever feel all these things in this book are not new to us.

Get this one thing from this book. Your Consciousness travels with you to the next life.

It is very important to treat your soul with respect. You are unhappy because you are putting your Atman down to make others happy. When you realize this one fact you will live your life in your zone and attract divine energy. This is not selfish, this is selfless. The journey is yours and you have to choose that wisely.

We are in an amazing era because of technology and tons of information at our fingertips. Everyone shares something and we don't know whether it's good or bad and we act on our thoughts based on the information we take into our brains.

Don't judge others at the same time you make choices on whom you interact with, what to watch and what not to watch. How we do with food the same way, what we put in our brain. You are a masterpiece, and cherish every moment on this earth. No one ever existed before like you and no one in the future. You are unique.

Whatever you have, try to give back as much as you can to others.

It may be a small book or some thoughts. Leave it to the next generations.

God didn't make anyone special. He created everyone equal.

CHAPTER 7

Shift focus

Every human has a story, they thrive to be a hero in their story and that story is only right for them. I learned in my midlife about self-love. I was making mistakes putting myself down and giving importance to others. That gives happiness to others and when I change back giving importance to my soul. Some people thought I have mental issues, some people were wondering, where did she get this courage from and others enjoyed and supported me. Do what feel good to you?

I tell myself again and again that I love myself. It sounds weird. I don't wait for others to accept me, like me or love me. I love myself to the core. My importance is to my soul. When I give this importance to my soul, my body is connected to it, so I have to take care of it and my mind is also connected to it.

I have to be conscious of what I put in my body and mind. What do I eat? Whom do I meet? What do I watch? love other humans without judgment, more observant. Walk away from things that don't serve you. Your soul becomes light and enters a higher power. I don't know what that is but it is there. Don't be afraid of anything, anyone. Your goal is to get control of your light and train the light to merge smoothly when you leave this body and that training can be done when you are in the body. Giving back gives satisfaction and happiness. These are small lessons from a middle-aged woman who never believed in herself and was complaining about her surroundings and got tired of that life took Incharge of her life and started working hard until I got the results. Today I am proud enough to say that we have three employees and started a business without any help myself and made six figures consistently selling Real estate in 2021 and 2022.

End of Achieve what you want

I'm finishing this book to achieve what you want. I enjoyed talking about my life and myself. I can't say that I'm very successful, but you know what, every day I have my doubts, but I just ignore them and then work and focus on my work and see what I can do to grow. So, that's what I'm doing and why I want people to read this book because as an immigrant, I came to this country and my childhood was not very great. I had a rough childhood and was abusive, most of the time I was down because of my skin color, and then, I went to college, and I got my degree. I had dreams and people said that I am incompetent. That's what people stamped on my face and then I pulled myself and just with some support. I imagined a person and thought that he believed and held my hand and said I could do whatever I am capable of.

I don't know if it's my imagination. That's what I expected from my family as well, which did not happen. That's a part of our life. When things don't work out, we need to move on and have faith in ourselves.

Whatever internal desires you have, that is your life purpose. If you are good at heart, you will figure it out. So, with that, I end this to achieve what you want. And this book is dedicated to my friend whom I don't know if I imagined him or he's there, but whoever is helping me to stand up on my own feet. Uh, I'm grateful to them, and this book is dedicated to them. Thank you.

www.ingramcontent.com/pod-product-compliance
Lightning Source LLC
LaVergne TN
LVHW050336160826
845677LV00014B/3632

* 9 7 9 8 8 3 7 7 0 8 4 8 0 *